THEY LOVED
THEIR ENEMIES

PEACE·AND·JUSTICE·SERIES 3

THEY LOVED THEIR ENEMIES

True Stories of African Christians

MARIAN HOSTETLER

HERALD PRESS
Scottdale, Pennsylvania
Kitchener, Ontario

Library of Congress Cataloging-in-Publication Data

Hostetler, Marian, 1932-
  They loved their enemies.

  (Peace and justice series ; 3)
  Bibliography: p.
    1. Nonviolence—Religious aspects—Christianity—
Case studies.   2. Evil, Non-resistance to—Case studies.
3. Christians—Africa—Case Studies.   I. Title.
II. Series.
BT736.6.H67   1988   251.8'096   87-29696
ISBN 0-8361-3456-7 (pbk.)

THEY LOVED THEIR ENEMIES

*To those faithful Christians
whose stories are told here,
and to the many more
whose stories may not be known to us,
but are to God.*

Contents

Foreword

Human beings normally respond to violence with violence. Because this action is often shaped by our beliefs, it says a lot about us.

The Hebrews of the Old Testament era met violence with violence. "An eye for an eye and a tooth for a tooth," was the principle they followed (Exodus 21:24).

Jesus gave a new commandment in the New Testament: Do not take revenge on someone who wrongs you. "If anyone slaps you on your right cheek, let him slap your left cheek, too" (Matthew 5:39).

He then went a step further. He commanded his disciples, "Love your enemies and pray for those who persecute you so that you may become the children of your Father in heaven" (Matthew 5:44b-45a).

This commandment, "love your enemies" became the guiding light for the early Christians and for many believers since then. Needless to say, it is often a costly commandment to obey.

In this book, the author shows how African Christians suffered and quite often died rather than fight their enemies. In some cases, love for enemies turned them into disciples of Jesus.

In *They Loved Their Enemies*, author Marian Hostetler has compiled a few of the many stories of African Christians who overcame evil with good.

Her book is number three in the Peace and Justice Series listed at the back of the book. For further reading on this theme, check the sources listed near the end of the book.

—J. Allen Brubaker, Editor
Peace and Justice Series

Preface

Christians have been present in Africa since New Testament times. Through all these hundreds of years, believers have been mocked, persecuted, even killed because of their faith. Some of these Christian Africans have met their enemies in the spirit lived and taught by Jesus Christ: "Love your enemies and pray for those who persecute you. Father, forgive them . . . ." (See Matthew 5:44; Luke 23:34.)

In this collection of true stories you will find people young and old, male and female, leaders and ordinary folk. All of them followed Christ's way of love. You will find stories of people from 1,700 years ago and those from recent years. You will find stories from Algeria to South Africa, from Sierra Leone to Kenya.

Surely there are many, many more stories. Those included here come from a variety of times and places.

The stories from the early days of the church come from North Africa, because that is where the Christians lived at that time. Christianity soon disappeared from most of North Africa because of persecution, fighting among themselves, and the coming of Islam.

For nearly a thousand years, Christianity in Africa survived only in Egypt and in Ethiopia. The few stories we have from that time come from Egypt.

In the 1500s and later, European explorers along the coast of Africa established forts and trading centers. Some attempted mission work, but with no lasting results. The church in sub-Sahara Africa had its beginnings in the 1800s when missionaries arrived from Europe and North America. For this reason, most of our stories come from the last 200 years.

These stories should help us realize that Jesus' way of love, peace, and forgiveness was not just for him (and Stephen and Paul), but for all of his disciples. May the examples of these Christians in Africa be an inspiration to us.

This book is number three in a series on peace and justice themes. It shows how African Christians faced conflict and lived out the teachings of Jesus. Other titles in the series appear inside the back cover. For more about Christians who loved their enemies, check the sources listed in the back of the book.

—*Marian Hostetler*

CHAPTER 1

I Am a Christian

In the year 203 it was dangerous to be a Christian in Tunisia. That year, a 22-year-old mother named Perpetua was arrested. Also arrested were her pregnant slave, Felicity, Felicity's brother, and two other young men. They were arrested because they were Christians and therefore refused to worship the Roman emperor as Roman citizens were required to do.

Perpetua's father came to prison to visit her. He tried to persuade her to give up her faith. "Father," she said, "do you see that clay jar?"

"Yes," he answered.

"Can it be anything else besides a jar?"

"No."

"Well, neither can I be anything else than what I am—a Christian."

Her father became so furious that he began to strike her. He saw that this would do no good, so he gave up and left.

The five Christians were then transferred to the big prison in Carthage, a place so crowded with prisoners that they could scarcely breathe. Some Christian friends paid the guards so Perpetua could sometimes go out into the prison courtyard. There she could move and breathe. She could also talk with her mother and brother when they came to visit her. And best of all, she could nurse her hungry baby boy whom they brought along.

Her father came to see her once more and said, "Daughter, consider my white hair. I raised you. I loved you more than your brothers. Don't ruin my name in front of everyone. Think of your mother and your aunt. Don't destroy our family!" Then he kissed her hands and knelt before her, tears in his eyes. Perpetua could only say, "At the trial, it will be as God wills. Our life depends on him, not on ourselves."

At last the time came for her to appear before the judge. Her father also appeared there with her baby. "At least have pity on your child!" he cried out to his daughter.

"Yes," said the judge. "Think of your young son and of your old father. Make a sacrifice to the emperor and go free."

"I cannot do it," answered Perpetua. "I am a Christian."

Then they ordered her father, still standing there, to be whipped. When they struck her aged father, Perpetua felt as if she were being whipped herself.

Then the judge sentenced the five Christians to death by wild animals. Killing prisoners this way was a part of the games the Romans loved to watch in their stadiums.

Just three days before the games, Felicity, the slave girl, gave birth to a daughter in prison. She gave up her baby to a Christian woman who agreed to raise her as her own daughter. On March 7 of the year 203, the condemned prisoners joyfully left the prison for the stadium. They were rejoicing because that day they would be with the Lord in heaven. Leading the way was a slave carrying a sign with their names and their crime: "They say they are Christians."

The men were thrown to the beasts first. A leopard and a bear attacked the first two, and a wild boar tore apart the third. Then the two women, stripped of their clothing and held fast by nets, were led out to be attacked by a maddened cow.

When the blood-thirsty crowd saw frail Perpetua and Felicity, who had just had a baby, they became ashamed of themselves. Their shame, however, was not great enough to ask for the prisoners' freedom. They only demanded that they be allowed to wear clothing.

When reclothed, they were brought back to the arena. The cow attacked Perpetua first, throwing her into the air. She landed on her back, then painfully got up. She saw Felicity, her servant, but also her sister in Christ, lying on the ground. She went to help her.

The two wounded women stood up together. The crowd decided that these brave women could be spared from death by the wild animals. Soldiers would kill them instead.

As they left the arena, Perpetua saw her brother in a group of Christians. She cried out to them, "Be faithful. Love each other. Don't be ashamed of our death for our faith."

Soon all five prisoners, injured and bloody, were brought back into the arena so the crowd could watch soldiers with flashing swords slash their throats. The prisoners said farewell to each other with the Christian greeting, the kiss of peace. Then they stood silently, ready to die.

CHAPTER 2

Who Really Has the Power?

For over 100 years, from 180-313, the Roman emperors killed and persecuted Christians in North Africa. Some Christians were carried off as slaves to work in copper and silver mines near Constantine (now in Algeria). Often their masters whipped these mine workers or put out one of their eyes or shaved their heads or branded them on the forehead with a red-hot iron.

Some slaves were chained to each other by their ankles. Others had their neck chained to their feet so they couldn't stand up straight.

Cyprian, a North African church leader, had been exiled from Carthage to a small village because of his work. From there he wrote to these Christian slaves to encourage them. He said, "Before being put in the mines, you were beaten. But a wooden club doesn't frighten a Christian, for our hope is also in the wood of the cross. They chained you hand and foot, hurting you. But God is in you and you have courage—so your chains are not bonds but like bracelets made by the Lord. They will not let you wash yourselves, so outwardly you are dirty, but inside you are pure and clean. You are cold because you don't have enough clothing, but the person who has 'put on' Christ is well-dressed. You cannot celebrate the offering of holy communion, but your lives are a precious offering and sacrifice, holy and acceptable to God, just as the apostle Paul wrote to the Christians at Rome."

Then in September of the year 258, Cyprian himself was arrested by two officers. Only one of them stayed to guard him during the night. Many of Cyprian's friends came and urged him to escape with their help. "No," he said, "I won't save myself. Or rather, I'll save myself—for eternal life. If I give up the fight, others might be led to do the same."

He looked at his visitors. "Why are you weeping?" he asked. "I won't be going to death, but to victory. My words to you are, don't bring trouble on yourselves. Be good citizens. We accept the emperor and the empire. But we refuse their gods."

The next morning when Cyprian was brought to court, the questioning began. "Are you, Cyprian, the leader of these ungodly people called Christians?"

"I am."

"The holy emperors have ordered you to offer sacrifices to our gods."

"I will not do it."

"You have been following this ungodly way for a long time and have led many others into this error. You are a notorious criminal. So you are going to be made an example of, to warn those that you have led astray. You are sentenced to be beheaded by the sword."

"I praise God," was Cyprian's response. The news quickly spread to the crowd waiting outside. The Christians shouted, "We're all Cyprians! Kill us with him!" Even many of the non-Christians were angry about the sentence. They remembered how Cyprian had worked tirelessly during a recent epidemic. He had risked his own life to take care of the sick and had organized the people to help each other.

Cyprian was led out from the court to a field where he was to be executed. He knelt and prayed. Then he stood and handed his cloak to the deacons who were with him and waited, dressed only in his tunic.

As the executioner walked up to him, Cyprian said to his deacon, Pontius, "You are to give this man 25 pieces of silver for his trouble." Then Cyprian blindfolded himself, and knelt down again, his head bowed so the executioner could easily strike the blow to behead him.

We know all this because Pontius the deacon wrote down what he saw that day. At the end of his account, he wrote, "The date was September 14, 258. The place was Carthage. The emperor was Valerian, and the provincial governor was Galarius the Great. But the one who really has the power is our Lord Jesus Christ." (See Acts 2:36; Philippians 2:11.)

CHAPTER 3

God's Soldiers

About 30 years after the death of Cyprian, the whole Roman Empire was celebrating the emperor's birthday. In Tangier (in what is now Morocco) a certain Marcellus was not celebrating.

Now Marcellus was a centurion in the Roman army. (A centurion was an officer over 100 men.) He had become a Christian, a soldier of Jesus Christ. How could he keep his oath to serve the emperor? he wondered. How could he earn his living by killing others? He therefore decided he could no longer be a soldier for the Roman emperor.

So instead of celebrating, Marcellus carried out the decision he had made. He stood in front of his hundred men, took off his soldier's belt and the badge showing his rank, and spoke to them. "I am a Christian. I can no longer serve the emperor."

In July of the year 289, Marcellus was brought before Fortunatus, the governor of the province. Fortunatus wanted to hush up the affair, but since Marcellus had publicly proclaimed his faith and his resolve to quit the army, he had no choice. He had Marcellus arrested.

The last of October, Marcellus was brought to trial before Judge Agricola.

"Are you guilty of this deed you are accused of?" demanded Agricola.

"Yes," answered Marcellus.

"What madness has made you break your oath as an officer and has led you to believe this Christian foolishness?"

"It is not foolishness to fear God."

"But you have laid down your weapons!"

"Yes, because it is not good for a Christian who serves Christ to serve other powers as well," Marcellus answered.

The judge sentenced him to death by beheading. Before leaving for his execution, Marcellus said one more thing to the judge.

"May God bless you, Agricola."

Six years after this, another birthday celebration was going on near Tebessa in what is now Algeria. This was not a celebration for the birthday of the emperor, but for the 21st birthday of a young man, Maximilian.

His father, Fabius Victor, was proud of his fine son. As a recruiter for the Roman army, Fabius had planned a special birthday surprise for Maximilian. He had told Dion, the area commander, that his son would be joining the army. Furthermore, he had had special clothes made for his son as part of his uniform.

Instead of happiness, which Fabius thought his surprise would bring to his son, his announcement brought sadness.

"You know, Father," Maximilian said, "I have become a Christian and my Lord says I am to love my enemies. How can I become a soldier? It is impossible!"

Fabius was horrified. "Son, I'm sorry," he said. "I didn't realize that being a Christian would keep you from serving in the army. But I have already given the commander your name, and tomorrow you will have to go to enlist. Otherwise, you can be sentenced to death."

"I will go with you to see the commander tomorrow, but I will not join the army," Maximilian answered.

The next day, the commander Dion tried to convince the young man that he was wrong. "There are other Christians in the army, I'm told. They don't mind."

"They know what is right for themselves, but I know what is right for me. I will not be a Roman soldier. I am already a soldier of my God," Maximilian replied.

"Don't be foolish," said Dion. "Let me put this soldier's badge on you, and I will forget that you said you were a Christian. That's a crime in itself, you know."

"If you place the soldier's badge on me, I will remove it, because I already wear Christ's badge. I serve him, and it is he that I will follow."

So the commander pronounced the sentence. "You are condemned to death by beheading."

"Thank you, Lord," said Maximilian.

He spoke some of his last words to his father as they walked to the place of execution. "Please, Father," he requested, "take the new clothes which you prepared for me and give them to the soldier who will kill me."

The church honored Maximilian by burying his body beside that of their leader, Cyprian, who had given his life for the Lord 37 years before. Both served as good soldiers of Jesus Christ. (See 2 Timothy 2:3.)

CHAPTER 4

Where Is "Abba"?

The leader or patriarch of the Coptic Church in Egypt for over 45 years (from 326-372) was Abba (Father) Athanasius. Earlier, the Roman emperors had accepted Christianity, but now disagreements among Christians had brought persecution and distress to the church. Some who had strayed into false beliefs were trying to force others to accept these beliefs. Some of the emperors agreed with these false teachings.

Several Roman soldiers came to Abba Athanasius and told him to leave his churches and his land and go into exile. He refused because he had a written permit from the emperor saying that he could stay. But when ordered again to leave by a second group of soldiers, Athanasius realized that he was in danger. He therefore asked the Christians to fast and pray.

One evening as the people were in church worshiping and praying, they heard a noise outside. The church doors burst open and soldiers marched in, trampling on people and shooting arrows at them.

Abba Athanasius, seated in front of the church, asked his

deacon to read Psalm 136. He asked the people to say in response to each verse, "For God's mercy endures forever."

The people stood. While they chanted those words of faith, their bodies formed a living barrier between the soldiers and their beloved leader. Some of the monks quietly gathered around Athanasius and carried him away. By the time the soldiers had hacked their way through the people, the one they had been ordered to capture dead or alive had vanished.

Another time the authorities ordered Athanasius to leave Alexandria. He decided to do this rather than endanger his people. As he prepared to sail up the Nile River, he gathered the people together and said, "Don't let your hearts be troubled. This is only a passing cloud." He and his companions then set sail.

Unknown to Athanasius, the prefect who commanded the Roman soldiers had ordered his men to follow Athanasius. Along the way, Athanasius had his sailors stop for a rest under a palm tree along the riverbank. Suddenly Athanasius said, "We're not going to continue upstream. We're going back to Alexandria to prove that he who protects us is greater than he who persecutes us."

So they boarded the boat, turned it around, and headed back toward Alexandria. They had gone only a few miles when they met the prefect's boat. The sailors called out, "Have you seen Athanasius and his men?"

Athanasius, sitting among his friends, with a hood half hiding his face, answered, "He's not far away!" The prefect's sailors began to row faster, going upstream, while Athanasius and his men continued downstream to Alexandria. He arrived there safely and lived there for some time in security because the prefect didn't know where he was.

Not long after this, in the late 300s, another emperor ordered all the bishops of the church to leave the country. One evening one of the bishops, Abba Melas, was working in his church. As he cleaned and lighted the lamps, a group of soldiers came to take him into exile. It never occurred to them that the "servant" doing such lowly tasks could be the bishop. They commanded him, "Take us to Abba Melas."

Abba Melas told them, "The bishop will be informed of your coming." Then he led them to his own house. There he prepared supper for them and served it to them himself. After they had eaten as much as they wished, he said, "I am Abba Melas."

They were so touched by his kind ways and his humility that they offered him the chance to escape.

"No," he said, "I would rather be banished for the truth than to be free without the truth." (See John 8:31-36.)

CHAPTER 5

The Loving Bandit

Moses the Black was such an unruly slave that his Egyptian owner, who couldn't control him, sent him away. So about the year 400, the banished Moses went to a desert region where he lived as an outlaw. Being a strong leader, he soon attracted 70 other bandits to his gang. Their killing and robbery terrorized everyone in the area and any travelers passing by.

Moses was huge. Rumor had it that he could eat a whole sheep and drink a whole jar of wine at one time. Besides food, he liked women and killing people.

However, Moses the Black sometimes wondered about God. He would look at the sun and say, "Oh, Sun, if you are God, tell me. I don't know you, God. Show yourself to me."

One day as he prayed this way, a voice told him, "Go to the desert of Wadi Natrun. The holy men there will tell you about God."

The monks at Wadi Natrun were afraid at first when they saw this huge man with his sword, but they began to teach him. Moses learned eagerly and happily and soon was baptized. He lived in a cell alone, near the other monks, and tried to make up for his many past sins by living a good life. He changed so much that the other 500 brothers chose him to be their leader and he became a priest.

As Moses was talking to his monks one day, some people passing by mocked him and spoke many abusive words about him. Moses said nothing.

Later the monks asked him, "Weren't you bothered by what those people said?"

"Yes, I was," answered Moses. "But a true follower of Christ needs to learn to be calm in his body and calm in his soul. When someone is mocked and yet controls his tongue, he has a calm body. When the one who is abused doesn't even feel anger, then he has a calm soul."

Once a brother was found guilty of a serious sin. The others, who were gathering to judge him and to decide on his punishment, sent word to Moses to join them.

When they saw him walking toward them, he was carrying on his back an old heavy basket filled with sand.

"What are you doing? What in the world is that?" they called to him.

Moses answered, "If I'm coming to judge another, I need to remember how heavy my own sins were, even though I no longer bear them."

With this example and reminder, the monks forgave their guilty brother and told him to go and sin no more.

CHAPTER 6

Peace and Persecution

After the followers of Muhammad conquered Egypt in the year 642, the church passed through times of peace and times of persecution. Whether the church would suffer persecution depended upon the character and whims of the various Muslim rulers. Incidents from the life of Patriarch Abba Mattheos, who led the church from 1378-1409, illustrate those "ups and downs."

In Cairo, a mob was preparing to burn a certain monastery. Now Sultan Barquq was a good ruler. When he heard of this, he sent four Islamic judges to prevent the burning. The judges were able to disperse the crowd, but the angry mob decided to burn another monastery.

Abba Mattheos heard what was happening and arrived at the monastery first. As the rioters came near, he faced them and called out to them. "Whoever dares, let him take his sword and kill me. Because here I stand, and I will let no one enter." The mob, astonished at his bravery, retreated.

Later, Sultan Barquq was forced out of power by two princes who had a plan to harass the Christians. One of the princes called Abba Mattheos before him. He demanded that Mattheos hand over the treasures and wealth of the church. Mattheos refused, and the surprised prince let him go.

When Abba Mattheos heard that the second prince was preparing a campaign of persecution against the Christians, he went to him and rebuked him sternly. The furious prince pulled out his sword. Mattheos calmly turned his neck toward the prince and said, "Kill me, then." The astounded prince let Mattheos leave in peace.

Later these two princes were deposed. Sultan Barquq returned and there was a time of peace again. However, the peace ended when Barquq died and cruel Sultan Sodon took his place. Hearing that the sultan had a plot to massacre the Christians, Abba Mattheos went to the church and prayed for seven days. In a vision he heard, "God has heard your prayers, and the enemy's plans will be brought to nothing."

Mattheos went home rejoicing. When he arrived, there was a message from Sultan Sodon that he urgently wished to see him.

The Sultan said to Mattheos, "Something inside me made me call you here to tell you that I have been plotting to kill the Christians."

Abba Mattheos answered, "God is the fortress of his people. No matter how powerful a sultan is, he cannot hurt God's people except by God's permission." Then Abba and his people gathered together to offer thanks to God for their deliverance.

However, the man second in power was Prince Ozbek. He hated the Christians and killed or imprisoned as many as he could. Abba Mattheos begged him to let the people live in peace, but the prince stubbornly ignored him.

Mattheos went to his church again, praying for help for his persecuted people. At the end of six days, he received the news that Prince Ozbek had been stabbed and killed.

Then came a time of peace, followed by yet another time of ruthless persecution under a new leader, Prince Gamal. Mattheos prayed intensely for the church, but by now, he was so frail and old that he became ill.

The prince decided to require that Abba Mattheos pay an extra tax of a half million dinars. The Christians gave all they could to raise this outlandish sum and were able to present the money to the prince for their beloved leader.

When he received the money, Prince Gamal became even more arrogant and rude. He sent a messenger to Abba Mattheos saying, "You must come to see me in person!"

Mattheos, sick in bed, smiled happily and told the messenger, "I can't come today. Come for me tomorrow."

Abba Mattheos could smile because he knew that he would die that day and go to be with the Lord. Besides the Christians, many Muslims and Jews loved and honored him and regretted his death.

CHAPTER 7

They Found the Way

The people on the island of Madagascar in the early 1800s faced slavery, poverty, and a lack of schools and education. When young Radama I became king, he wanted to do all he could to help his people to a better life. One of the first things he did was to ask the English to send people to help him achieve his goals.

The English missionaries who came to Madagascar at his request found much to do. They wrote down the language of the people, started the first schools on the island, and began to translate the Bible.

By 1828, things in Madagascar had begun to change. Some of the people had become Christians. They had Bibles in their own language, and the relationship between masters and slaves was better. Before he could accomplish more, 36-year-old King Radama died. Ravalona, one of his wives, took over the throne.

Queen Ravalona and her advisers did not like the changes which were taking place. They wanted to keep the old religion of ancestor worship. They wanted to continue using sorcery and witchcraft to strengthen their position as rulers. Queen Ravalona wanted to get rid of Christianity, too, since it was foreign to their old ways. She declared anyone who taught against sorcery a traitor.

On March 2, 1835, Queen Ravalona called the people together. Eighty thousand of them gathered to hear the royal decree, which stated, "The Christian religion is forbidden everywhere on the island. Christians will have one month to repent of their white religion."

To assure that the decree was carried out, Ravalona sent spies everywhere. She also organized a royal army and encouraged the people to denounce anyone they suspected of being a Christian. Since the queen had forced the English missionaries to leave her kingdom, the Christians were on their own. But they had God and their Bibles. They were not fearful, but they were careful. They began meeting in secret, sometimes in forests, sometimes in caves, but never at the same place twice. They had to read their Bibles in secret, too, for the queen burned any that were found.

Two years after Queen Ravalona's decree, the Christian church was still flourishing. Then someone denounced a young Christian woman named Rasalama, and she was sentenced to die.

As she was being led to the hilltop where she was to be killed, she sang this song:

> I found the way, and I'm walking in it.
> I received salvation, and I'm keeping it.
> O Holy Spirit, help me.

At the place of execution, Rasalama asked permission to pray. As she was praying, the queen's soldiers killed her with their javelins. One of the people who saw her die said,

"If I could die as peacefully and as well as she did, I would gladly give my life for the Savior."

Rasalama was the first Christian in Madagascar to die for her faith. Some were later stoned to death. Some were burned. Some were forced to drink poison. Others, when they refused to renounce the Lord, were rolled up in straw mats and thrown off the hilltop near the queen's palace to the rocks below.

However, the church did not disappear. Each Christian's death brought others to believe in Christ. Even the queen's only son became a Christian. During the 30 years that Queen Ravalona persecuted the church, she killed several thousand Christians. But many thousands of others became believers.

CHAPTER 8

God's Slaves

In the delta region of Nigeria in the 1870s, the majority of the people were slaves. As Christianity began to spread here, the village chiefs did all they could to keep their slaves from following this new religion. If slaves did become Christians, the chiefs tried to force them to go against their beliefs. They made them work on Sundays or eat meat sacrificed to other gods.

One of the chiefs, called "Captain Hart," was especially cruel. His wife hated Christians. He ordered Joshua, one of his slaves who was a Christian, to eat meat from a pagan sacrifice. When Joshua refused, Captain Hart punished him for his disobedience. The chief's men threw him high into the air and let him fall to the ground. They did this again and again until his body was bruised and broken. His spirit, however, was not broken.

They argued with him, pleaded with him, and threatened him. Joshua said, "If my master requires me to work for him, I will do my best no matter how hard the work. But if he requires me to eat things sacrificed to gods, I will never do it."

So Joshua was sentenced to death. They tied his hands and feet, put him in a canoe, and paddled out into the river to drown him. As they went, Joshua prayed, "Forgive them for they know not what they do."

Captain Hart shouted at Joshua, "Are you praying again?" Then he grabbed Joshua and threw him into the water. When Joshua came to the surface, the chief's men pulled him into the canoe. Captain Hart gave him one more chance to renounce his faith and save his life.

Joshua chose to cling to his faith, so the chiefs threw him back into the water. When his body rose, they struck him on the head with their paddles and pierced his body with a sharp pole until he died.

In 1876, five slaves refused to take part in pagan sacrifices because they were Christians. As a result, their chief put them in chains and forced them to live in the forest for months.

One of them said, "It is impossible for me to return to the old ways of paganism. Jesus has put a padlock on my heart, and he has kept the key!"

Two years after that, another slave died of hunger because he would not eat meat which had been offered as a sacrifice. Others were tied to stakes on the ground and left for the ants to eat. Finally the chiefs decided to scatter the Christian slaves, separating them from each other and from their place of worship. This only helped to spread Christianity!

After Captain Hart's wife died, he changed. He let his slaves worship as they wished. Before his death, he threw his own fetishes in the river and received baptism.

Other things were happening about this time on the other side of Africa, in Kenya. David Koi's church sent him to a church center near Kilifi as a Bible teacher. A group of former slaves who had settled at Fulodoyo asked David to come to their village to teach them. David had barely begun his work in Kilifi, so he asked his church. They agreed that he should leave to go to the settlement of former slaves.

In 1883, several slave owners came to David's home. David suspected that they were up to no good, but he treated them with Christian courtesy. As they entered his home, David said, "Let's pray together." He knelt and prayed for God to bless these visitors and to guide their conversation together.

The slave owners began to question him about the former slaves who were living there at Fulodoyo. David Koi explained, "I don't encourage slaves to try to escape from their owners. Those who do come here are free to do their own work and care for their own gardens."

The men glared suspiciously as David continued. "My only work here is to teach the Bible. The church has sent me, and these people pay me nothing. I am here only to help them."

Now the men were becoming angry. They said to each other, "We can't believe that a man who has such training and ability is here only to help these former slaves. He's trying to deceive us."

"What do you teach these people?" one of them demanded.

"I teach the people the gospel of Jesus Christ, as it's told to us in the Bible." David began to tell the slave owners how he himself knew Jesus and had faith in him.

This was too much for the slave owners. If people began to believe such things, slavery would soon be destroyed, they thought. They decided to do something to frighten their own slaves so badly they would never try to escape.

Some of the slave owners rushed outside and dug a hole deep enough for a man to stand upright in it. Into this hole they put David so only his head and shoulders were visible above the ground. Then they beheaded him.

CHAPTER 9

You Can't Burn Our Souls

Mwanga, 20-year-old king of Uganda, was an evil and cruel person. Christianity had come to Uganda only a few years before. Still, there were many believers, including a number of young men from among the king's servants. The chief of the king's 200 servants, Joseph Mukasa, was a Christian.

Now the king liked to involve himself with his servants in homosexual activities. So Joseph warned the young Christians, "If the king tries to get you to do wrong things with him, refuse." Joseph tried to hide any of them that the king had his eye on.

King Mwanga discovered what was happening and was furious that the Christians would not do as he wished. His prime minister, Katikiro, also hated Christians. He hated Joseph especially because he had foiled a plot that Katikiro was planning against the king.

This was Katikiro's chance to get even, so he urged the king to get rid of Joseph. The king didn't need much persuading, and Joseph was condemned.

On November 15, 1885, just before the executioner cut

off his head, Joseph gave him a message for the king. "Katikiro is having me killed unjustly. I forgive him, but he had better change his way of life!"

After the king had Joseph killed, he thought, "Now the other Christians will be afraid. There will soon be no more of them."

How wrong he was! The Christians feared that this was just the beginning of persecution. So they met each night in secret to pray and to be strengthened by each other and by God.

Each night more and more people joined them. In one week 105 new people were baptized!

One day about six months later, the king saw Mwafu, Katikiro's son. He asked him, "Where have you been?"

"I've been with Dennis Sebuggwawo, who takes care of your weapons."

"What were you doing there?" demanded the king.

"Dennis is my cousin, and he's teaching me about Jesus."

Dennis heard and saw what was going on and came to Mwafu's help.

"What is this?" the king shouted at him. "What have you been doing with Mwafu?"

"Teaching him religion."

"You know I've forbidden this, and yet you dare to teach this religion to my prime minister's son?" The furious king seized one of his soldiers' poisoned spears and thrust it into Dennis's throat. Dennis suffered all that night and died the next morning. He was 16 years old.

The king was determined to root out this religion. The next day he called all of his servants together and locked the doors. He said, "Those of you who are Christians, line up along that wall. The rest stay with me."

About 30 of his servants lined up along the wall.

"Are you Christians?" he asked.

"Yes," came the answer.

"You wish to remain Christians?"

"Yes," they answered with one voice.

"Then you'll all die!"

King Mwanga had them tied up, and that afternoon they began the 27-kilometer march to Namugongo, the hill of execution. Five of them didn't make it to Namugongo but were killed on the way. One was beaten with sticks, two were speared. One had his arm cut off, then his head. One had his hands cut off, then his arms, then his feet. Then pieces of skin were pulled off and he was left to die.

When the condemned slaves arrived at Namugongo, they had to wait seven days till everything was properly prepared. On the day of the executions, the guards tied each one up hand and foot, then rolled them up individually in reed mats. They lined up the rolled-up mats like logs in a row on top of a wood pile. Then they piled more wood over them.

The men who were to light the fire made fun of the Christians. "Let's light this fire and see if the God you believe in will save you from it!"

One Christian named Bruno called back, "You can only burn our bodies. You can't burn our souls!"

Then the torches touched the dry wood. Above the noise of the crackling flames came the sound of voices praying. The fire and smoke swept upward toward the sky.

It was Ascension Day, June 3, 1886. That same day the souls of the Uganda martyrs ascended to God.

CHAPTER 10

Don't Kill

Kaboo, born in Côte d'Ivoire (Ivory Coast) in 1872, was the son of a chief. His life as a prince was unhappy. In those days when a tribe fought and lost a battle, the losing chief had to give his oldest son as a hostage to the winning tribe. This was to make sure that the losers would pay the required amount of ransom to the winners.

When Kaboo was very young, his father lost a war, and Kaboo became a hostage. Soon his father could pay, and the tribe returned Kaboo. Later when it happened again, the tribe kept Kaboo for several years before his father could pay enough. They treated Kaboo so badly that he never would speak to anyone about what happened.

When Kaboo was about 15, he became a hostage once more. Twice his father came to the victorious chief with all the ivory, rubber, and kola nuts he could find. But the chief claimed it was not enough and would not release Kaboo. Instead, day after day, he had him beaten with a thorny poison vine.

At last, since it was impossible for his father to pay any more, they planned to kill the young prince. They decided to bury him up to his neck in the sand, and then lure the driver ants to come and eat him.

Just when they were ready to begin his torture, a light flashed about Kàboo, blinding his tormentors. A voice called to him, "Flee!" Kaboo escaped and ran through the forest. After weeks in danger from wild animals and snakes and hostile tribes, he found his way out of the forest. He had come to Monrovia, Liberia, a safe place where some of his own Kru tribe were living.

At Monrovia, Kaboo first heard about the God of the Bible. The Christians there told him of Paul's conversion and how God's light flashed around him and how God spoke to him. (See Acts 9:1-22.) Kaboo knew it was this same God who had rescued him. He gladly gave himself to God. When he was baptized, he received the name Samuel Morris.

Sammy learned all he could about God from the missionaries he knew, but it wasn't enough to satisfy him. Even though he had no money, he talked and prayed his way onto a ship. It was sailing to America where he could learn more about the Holy Spirit.

The ship stopped first at some African ports, but had many troubles and delays for repairs. When it was finally on its way across the Atlantic Ocean, the captain gave his crew extra liquor to celebrate. The celebrations ended in a big fight.

One man, a big brute from Malay in the Pacific Ocean, thought he had been insulted by some of the others. He seized his knife and rushed at them to kill them. Sammy stepped in front of him and said quietly, "Don't kill. Don't kill."

Sammy didn't know that this Malay hated all blacks. He

had been boasting to the rest of the crew that he was going to kill Sammy as he had killed other Africans before. Sammy was the only black aboard.

As Sammy stood before the man, the Malay raised his weapon. His chance had come to carry out his boast! Sammy steadily looked into the man's eyes, making no move to defend himself. Slowly, the Malay lowered his weapon and left the deck to return to his bunk.

Sometime later, the Malay became desperately ill and was dying. Sammy went to the man's bunk to pray for him. God healed the Malay—not only from his sickness, but in his mind and spirit. God changed his hatred to love for Sammy.

God used Sammy to minister among the crew of the ship, in the churches of America, and at Taylor University, the Christian college he attended. Sammy's body, weakened by many beatings and hardships, could not resist the cold winter weather. He died in 1893, after less than a year in America. He was only 20 years old.

Sammy Morris is still remembered at Taylor University. Many young people from there have gone to Africa as missionaries to carry out the work Sammy had been unable to do himself.

CHAPTER 11

Let There Be No Quarrels or Fights

In 1913, a man traveled from village to village along the coast of the Gulf of Guinea. He had a long white beard and was dressed in a flowing white robe. William Wadé Harris had come from Liberia. As he walked through Côte d'Ivoire and into the Gold Coast (Ghana), he preached to the people and baptized them.

Women dressed in white also traveled with him, singing and shaking their calabash rattles to call the people together. The people in the villages along the coast were curious. They came to see who these strangers were and to hear the strange words they were speaking.

Harris said, "You must repent. You must burn your fetishes and everything to do with witchcraft and sorcery. You must be baptized in the name of the Father, Son, and Holy Spirit."

As the people came to burn their fetishes and receive baptism, he taught them more of God's ways.

"Obey God's commandments," he said. "Don't work on

Sundays, but work hard the other days. Live peacefully in your families and between tribes. Let there be no quarrels or fights or armed struggles."

Harris had not always practiced what he was preaching now. In fact, only four years earlier he had helped to lead an armed uprising against the government.

The revolt failed, and Harris was put into prison. While there, he heard God speaking to him and calling him to be a prophet and preacher. He listened to God's call and became a changed person.

As he traveled, more and more people thronged to hear his preaching and to follow the ways of God. In scarcely more than a year, 100,000 of them repented, burned their fetishes, and received baptism. They tried to live peacefully as Harris had taught them.

At the very moment Harris was preaching peace, the French who were in power in Côte d'Ivoire were becoming involved in World War I. They were trying to make the Ivorians into soldiers for France. They wanted to force 1,000 of them to go to Europe and fight Germany. The French, therefore, did not want to hear preaching about peace. They became more and more afraid of Harris's influence over the people.

The French not only disliked Harris because he preached nonviolence, but also because he told the people not to work on Sundays. The colonists wanted their servants to produce for them seven days a week. The plantation owners wanted their workers to be on the job every day.

In December 1914, the French governor of Côte d'Ivoire sent a letter to his administrators. "You must rid your areas of such people as Harris and his helpers," he said.

"See that they are sent back where they came from."

The administrators not only arrested Harris and his women helpers, they ordered their soldiers to severely beat them even though they offered no resistance. They tore their clothes from them. They broke the bamboo cross that Harris always carried. They threw Harris and his helpers into prison.

So Harris was once more in prison—this time not for preaching rebellion, but for preaching peace.

His influence was so great that if he had preached rebellion or called on his followers for help, there would have been an uprising. But he told them, "Vengeance belongs to God."

After a month of prison, Harris and his helpers were sent by ship back to Liberia. Helen Valentine, one of his assistants, died there from the beating she had received.

The French were not satisfied with expelling Harris. They tore down or burned many of the meeting places which the new Christians had built.

Harris was never allowed to return to Côte d'Ivoire to visit the churches begun through his preaching. However, his followers did not forget what he taught about Christ's way of peace.

A religious education booklet published by the Harrist Church in 1956 includes these questions and answers:

Question: Must one help and love also his enemies?
Response: If someone says he is your enemy—even if he does you wrong—God alone has the right to punish him. As for you, you must continue to love and help him as a brother. No one has the right to punish his brother.
Question: And if the enemy strikes us or insults us?

Response: The prophet suffered humiliation and violence from the French authorities; never did he return a blow. On every occasion, you must show yourself superior to your enemy by the forgiveness which you grant him, even in spite of himself. (See Matthew 5:38-48.)

CHAPTER 12

You Must Baptize All My Wives

Modi Din was one of the first pastors in the church begun by the Basel Mission in Cameroon in 1886. When World War I broke out, Germany was the colonial power in Cameroon, and Modi and some others were put in prison. The authorities suspected them of sympathizing with Germany's enemies.

Modi and the other prisoners were chained together two-by-two. They had to bend over as they chopped down the brush to clear the area around the prison. If a prisoner tried to stand up, or if he fell behind the others, the guard would whip him.

Modi's partner was an old chief who was not used to such work and could not keep up with the others. Modi felt sorry for the old man who would often be whipped.

During one of these beatings, Modi stood up. "Who says you can beat this old man?" he asked. "Can't you see how hard it is for him to do this work? If you must whip someone, whip me. I'll do my work and his, too."

The astonished guard said, "What? You're a Douala man and you want to help a man from the forest and

47

receive his punishment?"

"We're all brothers in God's sight," answered Modi. "To him, there are no Douala men and no men of the forest. You think you can beat people without being held accountable? Well, go ahead and beat us. But there's a Father in heaven who is counting the blows you give, and one day he'll hold you responsible for each one."

The soldier and all the prisoners were impressed by Modi's words. From then on, the soldier behaved differently. He didn't beat the prisoners, and when one of them was lagging behind, he would say to Modi, "Tell him to move forward."

Sometime after the war, when Modi was no longer a prisoner, he sent a young man to teach the gospel in a village ruled by a violent chief. This chief always had to have his own way. After a year, Modi came to visit the catechist and to see how his work was going. He found that some of those who had been receiving instruction from the catechist were ready for baptism.

Among those he accepted for baptism the next day were two wives of the chief. These women were pleased and went home to tell the good news. However, this made the chief's other wives jealous, and they told him they wanted to be baptized, too.

The chief sent for Modi and demanded, "Is it true that two of my wives will be baptized tomorrow?"

"Yes," answered Modi.

"I want all of my wives to be baptized—not just two!" said the chief.

"How many wives do you have?" asked Modi.

"Forty-three."

"I cannot baptize all your wives."

"But I'm ordering you to do it!"

"I can only baptize the two who have been instructed and who have satisfactorily answered my questions about their faith."

"I understand," said the chief. "It's the catechist's fault! He hasn't taught my wives as he should have. I'll have him whipped. Then I'll dismiss him and you can send me a better one."

"It's not his fault if your wives are ignorant of Christianity," said Modi. "If it's anyone's fault, it's yours! It's you who forbid them to study and to attend church."

"You will baptize my wives tomorrow!" the chief shouted violently.

The catechist and the other onlookers were frightened. They feared that the chief would kill Modi. They whispered to him to give in.

Modi calmly replied to the chief, "You can issue all the orders you want. I won't do it, because it would be a sin."

The chief could not stand being contradicted. He shouted, "For the last time, baptize all my wives! If not . . . ." He made a slashing motion with his hand across his throat to show Modi that he would behead him.

Modi answered, "I'm in your power. If you want to cut off my head, do it. But know this. Your threats will never make me go against God's will. If you kill me, I have nothing to lose. In fact, I'll be better off! I'll no longer have to cross all these mountains to come to visit this village."

The chief had never before seen such courage and calm in the face of his threats. It made an impression on him. At last he said to Modi, "Until now you haven't interfered with me in my job as chief, so I won't interfere in your work either. Baptize whomever you wish tomorrow."

CHAPTER 13

Punished for Nothing

Simon Kimbangu was in prison for life. The colonial government of the Belgian Congo had pronounced this sentence on him in 1921. The rulers were afraid of this peaceful prophet of God because thousands of people were flocking to hear his teaching. One of his fellow prisoners, Majewa Apollo, told this story about Kimbangu. At the time of the story, Kimbangu had already been in prison for 25 years.

At the end of one of the long prison buildings were special cells. They were for prisoners who were receiving extra punishment. Some of these had rebelled against the government. Some were mentally ill from their suffering. Some had become like children.

However, one of the prisoners in these cells was different from all the others. His name was Simon Kimbangu.

I learned to know him because I worked in the prison kitchen and took those prisoners their food. Kimbangu's cell was one and one-third meters by two meters. Kimbangu had a cement platform to sleep on, a reed mat on the floor, and two prison blankets.

Kimbangu was a heavy man of medium height. His face was old and wrinkled, his head partly bald with graying hair.

How was he different from us other prisoners? He would take no part in our jealousies and our hatred, no part in our efforts to harm each other. When he wasn't locked up, he would go out each morning to greet each prisoner and shake his hand. When the others persecuted him, he remained calm and peaceful, showing no anger. We could not understand him, but we respected him. We never admitted it, but we knew that his attitude and actions lessened the poisonous feelings in our hearts.

Sometimes he would not eat the food I brought him, and once the prison director beat him for this. The meal following that, he ate his stew, but not the piece of meat in it.

The next day, I saw why. When the 200 prisoners who had been taken out to work in the early morning were being returned in the late afternoon, Kimbangu stood by his cell door. As each one walked by, he gave them a tiny piece of his meat.

Because he had shared his meat, the prison director sent the guards to take Kimbangu to the torture cell. We knew what happened when the guards took a prisoner there. The guards usually came back carrying the prisoner's body. This time the guards came back alone.

After three days, we saw the guards leading Kimbangu back to his own cell. He went and shook hands with each guard, thanking them! He shook hands with all the prisoners and greeted each of us. Then he went to the prison director's office and greeted him as well!

I could not understand this man! I would threaten someone with death to get a larger piece of meat. He gave his away to others! I did many wrong things, and when I was punished, I planned my revenge. He was punished for nothing and showed only good will to those who did it!

This contact with Kimbangu led to Majewa Apollo's conversion. Five years later, after 30 years in prison, Simon Kimbangu died. The church which had begun from his teaching before his imprisonment is now called the Church of Jesus Christ on Earth by Simon Kimbangu. It has continued to follow—as its leader did—Christ's way of love and peace. Here are two examples.

After Kimbangu's death, the government continued persecuting the church. In the early 1950s it uprooted 37,000 Kimbanguist families from their homes and sent them to other parts of the country. However, the church continued to grow—and so did persecution of it.

Finally in 1956, some 600 leading Kimbanguist residents of Kinshasa wrote a letter to the Belgian governor general. "We are suffering so much. Wherever we meet for prayer, we are arrested by your soldiers," they said. "In order not to burden the police with added work, we shall all gather unarmed in the stadium where you can arrest us all at once or massacre us."

While the letter was being delivered, thousands of Kimbanguists left their jobs and gathered peacefully at the stadium for arrest or death. The governor general was stunned. He could not grant them official recognition, but he did grant them "toleration," and they were neither arrested nor killed.

In 1964 after the independent Congo had become Zaire, the government army came to Kisangani to fight the Simba rebels. The Kimbanguist Christians of that place had a simple church made of posts stuck in the ground with a palm branch roof. As the fighting came closer and closer, 170 of the Kimbanguists gathered in their palm branch church to pray. Though they had refused to participate in any fighting, they now feared for their lives.

As the Simba rebels began to flee from the government army, they threw grenades and shot at the praying people. Some of the government soldiers were flying overhead in an army plane. When they saw the praying crowd, they thought it was a group of rebels and began firing on them, too.

What could the Christians do? They stayed there, shot at from every side. They were ready to die, but not willing to kill. They continued to pray.

At last a Belgian officer and some government soldiers arrived and demanded, "What are you doing there?"

"We are praying," they answered.

"Yes. Praying for the rebels, no doubt," sneered the officer.

"We're praying for all God's children and for peace," said the pastor, showing his Bible. The officer took it, looked at it, put it in his pocket, and ordered his men to go on their way.

During this whole time, no one was even wounded. The Kimbanguists knew God had protected them.

CHAPTER 14

You Killed My Sister

Nsiamindele was a little boy in Kikaka, Angola. While his father was working in a far away city, his mother, "Mama" Mavivana, was taken before the village chief to be judged. She was brought because her sister who lived with them refused to go with the old man her uncles had arranged for her to marry. The chief accused Mama of being a bad woman because she had not forced her sister to go with her husband.

Mama replied, "I told her she should go, but she refused. What can I do?"

The chief became angry and told Mama Mavivana that it was her fault. He sentenced her to hard labor, but said she must be whipped first. A policeman, carrying out the chief's orders, began to beat Mama. Little Nsiamindele grabbed the policeman's legs and tried to stop him, but he wasn't strong enough. The policeman beat Mama till she fell to the ground.

Tied to Mama's back was her baby daughter, Nsiamindele's only sister. The people watching discovered that the baby girl had died from the beating. When Nsiamindele saw this, he said to the policeman, "You killed my sister! When I'm big, I'll pay you back for what you did to my mother and my little sister."

Later, Nsiamindele's father died at the city where he had gone to work, and soon after, his mother died also. The orphan boy went to live with his aunt. Later he lived with an uncle who helped him go to a Christian school.

On December 4, 1932, in the town of Matadi, Nsiamindele received baptism. After he finished school, Nsiamindele worked as a teacher, then as the manager of a railroad dining car. One day after work, a friend informed him, "The man who killed your sister is here in Matadi!"

Nsiamindele remembered his vow. "I swore to kill this man, and now he's here," he thought. "This is the time for my revenge."

He tried to fight these thoughts, because now he was a Christian and belonged to Jesus Christ. To keep his vow would be a sin. Should he or shouldn't he kill his enemy? Finally, Nsiamindele told his problem to one of his father's relatives, Don Manuel Matu.

"My son, aren't you a Christian?" Don Manuel Matu said. "What did Jesus say about his enemies who nailed him to the cross?"

"Father, forgive them; for they know not what they do," answered Nsiamindele.

"That's the way we must forgive," said Don Manuel.

He asked Nsiamindele to read 1 Peter 3:12 from his Bible. "For the eyes of the Lord are upon the righteous, and his ears are open to their prayer. But the face of the Lord is against those that do evil." Then Don Manuel prayed for Nsiamindele.

The next day when he was reading his Bible, Nsiamindele noticed Matthew 5:7. "Blessed are the merciful, for they shall obtain mercy." He knew then what he must do. He invited the former policeman and Don Manuel to come to his home the next evening. That day he prepared food for his guests.

When his guests came, Nsiamindele said, "We'll talk after we've eaten, for our custom says, 'Don't talk to a stranger who is hungry.'"

When the meal was over, the former policeman said, "God is merciful. I never thought you would invite me here and let me eat with you as you have done."

"I'm glad you were brave enough to say that," said Nsiamindele. "Do you remember what happened when I was a little boy?"

"Yes. I remember."

"I promised then that I would kill you for having killed my little sister. Jesus has shown me that I must forgive you instead. And I pray that he will forgive you also."

"Do you believe this?" Don Manuel asked the former policeman.

"Yes, I do," the man answered. "And I would like to ask God's pardon for the evil I did. I didn't want to do it. But because I followed orders, I did this wrong."

Then Don Manuel prayed that Nsiamindele and the policeman might be able to forget the past. Happiness filled them both, and Nsiamindele's enemy became instead his good friend.

CHAPTER 15

You Must Swear the Oath

In Kenya, the Africans were rising up against the British government. "The white people have oppressed us long enough," cried the rebels. "It's time to kill them!" The rebels banded together in an organization called the Mau Mau. They demanded that all Kenyans join it and take the Mau Mau oath. "If you don't join us," they threatened the Christians, "we'll know you are traitors, and we'll kill you."

The Christians didn't know what to do. They wanted their country to be independent, but they had learned to love, not hate. They had learned that it was wrong to kill.

What should they do? Join the Mau Mau and disobey Christ, or refuse to join and die? It was the night of February 13, 1953. Before going to sleep, Samuel Mukoro prayed to the Lord for his protection.

At two in the morning, Sara Mukoro awakened to hear someone calling, "Samuel, Samuel." Then came a loud knocking at the door, and some Mau Mau men and women burst into their house.

"What do you want?" asked Samuel.

"Give us your money unless you want to die. Give us the

keys to your cupboards and chests!"

The couple handed over the keys and money. Some of the Mau Mau dug through the Mukoros' possessions, piling up what they wanted to take along. At the same time, one was slashing Samuel with his machete. Three times he struck him. Blood streamed over Samuel's face and he couldn't see. Then the men took a belt and tied his hands behind his back. Next, they attacked Sara, hitting her over the head and shouting, "Why did you smile?"

"Because I'm not angry at you for what you're doing," she answered. So they beat her even more and broke her little finger.

Samuel and Sara kept trying to explain their work. "We preach the gospel," they said. "We want everyone to know Jesus—blacks and whites."

"Yes, we know your kind," they answered. "You refuse to help us in our fight against the foreigners." They beat Samuel still more and told him, "You must swear the Mau Mau oath." This oath included touching or drinking blood.

"No. The blood of Jesus is enough for me," said Samuel.

They became even more furious. "Swear!" they said, time after time. And each time when Samuel answered, "No," he was struck again. Then they stabbed him in the back.

"Lord!" Samuel cried out.

"Why are you calling to the Lord?" the Mau Mau asked. Samuel did not answer. They suddenly stopped beating him, but took some of his blood and smeared it on his mouth, as if he had sworn the oath. This made him sick to his stomach, and he fell over. They picked him up, laid him on his bed, and cut the belt binding his hands.

Then Samuel's youngest daughter began to cry. The

rebels said to Sara, "Do you want her to be killed?"

"No!" said Sara.

"Then make her be quiet!" They were getting ready to leave, taking everything with them. Sara said to them, "Please, leave one cover for our little daughter. It's very cold." They threw one at her.

"And what am I to cover myself with?" asked Samuel. They brought him his cloth, but carried off everything else from the house except some underclothes.

As they left, they said, "We're going now, but don't forget to pray for us."

"We'll pray that the Lord will help you and save you," responded Sara and Samuel.

They did pray. They also praised the Lord, for during that whole time they were being beaten, they had felt neither worry nor despair. They praised him for saving them from death and for protecting their children. The children had seen everything, yet they had remained silent except for the crying of the youngest daughter.

They prayed for someone to come to help them. Their sister-in-law arrived, made them some tea, and bandaged their worst wounds. Not until morning were they sure that the raiding band was gone. Then Samuel and Sara went to the hospital.

Their prayers for those Mau Mau attackers were sincere. Samuel said later, "We meant it. If they had returned and asked us for a cup of tea, we would have done all we could to prepare one for them."

Sara was left with a crooked little finger. Samuel could never walk normally again because of a cut tendon in his ankle. But they were happy the Lord had helped them to be faithful to his way of love.

CHAPTER 16

Hymns Help

Beyena was a young Christian in Ethiopia in 1958. It was a time when the government was persecuting Christians.

When government soldiers came to Beyena's village, people told them that Beyena was one of the church leaders. To force him to give up his faith, the soldiers stuffed his nose with cow dung. Since this didn't persuade him, they put him on trial for insulting his country's religion. His own uncle, afraid of the soldiers, witnessed against him. Beyena was sentenced to prison for a year. After prison, Beyena went to Bible school to continue his studies. From there the church sent him to work in a village with only four Christians. A few months later, the four had increased to forty!

One of the new Christians was the husband of a woman who practiced sorcery. The unbelievers were furious that he had become a Christian. They made such an uproar that Beyena and two friends were arrested for disturbing the peace.

The Christians could do two things to obtain their

release. They had to give a gift of wine to the officials as a bribe. And they had to drink some beer as a sign they were sorry. They refused to do either. So the three were threatened with death. They were stripped of their clothes, chained, and placed in the cold water of a mountain spring. For three days of scorching sun, and three nights of icy cold, they lay naked in the water and oozing mud.

The fourth morning, people living near the spring could hear them singing hymns. Taking pity on them, the people appealed to the chief to put the young men in prison instead of torturing them this way.

At their trial, false witnesses said that all three had slandered the traditional religion and had taught against paying taxes. Then the judge told them they must deny their faith.

Instead, Beyena began to preach against sin to the people in the court. The furious guards beat the prisoners, and the judge sentenced them to two years in prison.

In prison, they continued to witness for Christ and to sing hymns. Because of their good conduct, they did not have to serve the whole two-year sentence. When they left the prison, they left something special behind them: ten new Christians!

Bekelatch attended a Christian girls' school six kilometers from her home. Each day she walked to school, carrying on her shoulders food for the noon meal. At this school, Bekelatch learned to know Jesus.

Then came the Adibar festival which marked the beginning of the Ethiopian new year. At that time, many families sacrificed a black sheep to Satan to ask his protection for the coming year.

As her family was getting ready for the festival, 12-year-old Bekelatch's father asked her to prepare some coffee.

"Is it for Satan?" she asked.

"Of course it's for Satan," he answered.

Bekelatch looked at her father. "I can't do it, Father," she said. "I belong to Jesus now, and I can't worship Satan."

Her father was so angry he made her leave home. He forbade her to return and said she would receive no more food from him.

Bekelatch continued going to school, but she didn't tell her teachers what had happened. Instead, she prayed to God, asking him to take care of her. And he did. Bekelatch had been friendly to an old woman on her way to school, and this woman gave Bekelatch food and a mat to sleep on at night.

When Bekelatch's father became seriously ill, he allowed her to return home to help out. One day as she was sweeping the house and humming a hymn, her father called to her from his bed. "Daughter, God took care of you when I wouldn't give you anything. You are right to follow Jesus. You can come back home to live with us."

CHAPTER 17

You Must Be Crazy

The 1963 constitution of Somalia said, "It is unlawful to spread any religion except Islam, the true religion." It was this law that led to Musa's arrest.

Musa, a Somali, had heard about Christ and had accepted him while he was in Ethiopia. He also received training there from a missionary doctor for dispensary work.

When Musa returned to Somalia, he worked in a dispensary. Even though it was illegal, he could not help telling others of his Savior while he worked. The news spread that there was an unusual person in town—a Christian Somali.

The police began to watch him closely to see if they could catch him preaching. A person that Musa considered a friend informed the police that Musa had a book in his house called *How to Lead a Muslim to Christ*. The police came to the dispensary and took Musa to his house. When they found the book, they arrested Musa and charged him with trying to destroy the religion of his country.

On the day of Musa's trial, 600 curious people filled the

courtroom. The judge said to him, "You are accused of being a Christian. What do you say to this?"

Musa stood and spoke in a clear voice, "It's true, Your Honor. I'm a disciple of Jesus, and I will remain one, even if you imprison me or kill me." This made the crowd angry. They began to stomp their feet, whistle, and call out, "Put him in prison!"

. Musa prayed silently, "Thank you, Lord, for letting me witness to you in this way."

The judge said, "Because you have admitted you're a Christian, because this book was found in your house, and because we've been told that you're trying to spread this religion, you are sentenced to six months in prison. Or you can pay a fine."

Musa could not pay his fine and so he went to prison. Usually when a person could not pay, his clan would free him by paying the fine for him. But Musa's clan sent this message to him: "If you were in prison for killing someone, we would pay your fine and have you released. But we can't do it for your crime. Such a crime has never been committed before."

The chief of another clan was also in prison for having led his clan in fighting an enemy clan. When he heard about Musa, the chief said to the other prisoners, "Let's get this 'unbeliever.' We'll make him do the dirtiest jobs." So on his first day in prison, they made Musa clean the toilets. The next day, they looked on in astonishment as Musa went and voluntarily cleaned the toilets.

The news spread: "There's a Somali in prison for saying in court that he's a Christian." The governor of the province came to the prison to see this strange case.

"How can a Somali be put in prison for being a Christian?" he asked. "You must be crazy!"

Musa spoke to the governor about his faith. When the governor left, he ordered that Musa be provided with medicines so that he could give medical care to the other prisoners.

Before long, the prison guards came to respect Musa. They even gave him all the prison keys so that he could go wherever necessary. He found that in prison he could do what he was forbidden to do on the outside—witness to his faith. He could speak of Jesus, not only to the other prisoners, but also to the important visitors who came to question him.

All this attention that Musa began receiving made his fellow prisoner, the old chief, even more angry. But Musa always treated him politely.

Then he discovered that the chief liked to know what was going on in the outside world. However, the chief couldn't read the newspaper which was printed in Italian. So Musa began sitting with him each day to read and explain the news to him.

"Musa," said his former tormentor one day, "if I get out of prison first, I'm going to pay your fine." And he did. Musa was freed, went back to his job at the dispensary, and saved his money so he could repay the chief.

CHAPTER 18

The Weapon of Love

Rwanda is a beautiful land of high mountains, deep valleys, rushing torrents, and blue lakes dotted with green islands. But from 1959 to 1962, life in Rwanda was painful because of violence, arson, looting, and lawlessness.

The Hutu, a hardworking farming tribe, had been dominated for 300 years by the Tutsi tribe who were proud and educated cattle-herders. When Rwanda was struggling to become an independent nation, the Hutu rebelled against the Tutsi and fighting broke out between them. In the midst of this violence, some Christians put Jesus above their tribe and nation.

In one area during the day, the Hutu burned the Tutsi houses. At night the Tutsi retaliated by burning the Hutu homes. People of both sides were either dying or becoming refugees. Many of the homeless fled to the church center of Pastor Daniel. Though old and suffering from asthma, the pastor did what he could to help the refugees.

One morning, Daniel was warned that a band of ruffians was coming to attack the refugees. He called the people from the school buildings where they were camping and assembled them in the church. When they were inside, Daniel locked the church doors and prayed to God for protection. Then he said to the people, "You are in God's house. No matter what happens, you must not fight."

The attackers arrived and tried to break down the doors. The thick wood was too strong for them, so they climbed up onto the roof and removed part of it. Three of them got inside the church and began to beat up the refugees. The crowd of refugees could easily have killed these few men.

Daniel, scarcely able to breathe because of his asthma, said to the refugees, "Remember, we are Christians. We can't fight."

The refugees allowed the attackers to kick and beat them. After a few minutes of hitting and kicking unresisting people, the attackers gave up, and shamefacedly left.

The weapon of love was stronger than the weapon of hate.

One old Tutsi Christian woman who lost everything when her home was burned had to flee to another area. Even though she knew she should forgive those who had destroyed her home, she was unable to do so. She felt she must have revenge.

One dark night, she found her way back to where she had lived. She knew who had burned her house, and she had with her a box of matches to set fire to their house. Quietly, she approached the house and slid open her matchbox. It was completely empty! She threw it down and fled again, this time arriving in a refugee camp in the neighboring country of Tanganyika, now Tanzania.

One day, two Hutu Christians came to the camp of Tutsi refugees. It was hard for them to come among their "enemies," but God wanted them to share his love with the Tutsi. One of those gathering around the visitors to listen to them was the old woman. She saw the love of Jesus in the visitors' faces and the unity between Hutu Christians and Tutsi Christians. Her heart softened.

The next day, she stood up in a meeting and told everyone, "I have repented of my hatred of the Hutu who burned my house. I praise the Lord that he kept me from destroying my enemy's house by seeing that my box of matches was empty."

CHAPTER 19

Love Is Powerful

When Sierra Leone became independent in 1961, the new government appointed Martha Bankura to be a women's tribal leader. She may have been chosen for this position because of the way she had handled some rioters a few years before.

People had been unhappy about the taxes they had to pay. Some of them who had drunk too much liquor began rioting. These rioters arrived at Gbendembu, Ya Martha's village, where they began to burn down the houses. Ya Martha could hear people crying and waiting as they saw their houses and possessions turning into smoke and ashes. So she decided she had better prepare for the rioters. When they arrived at her house, she was ready. She had a huge pan of cool water on the veranda and offered each of them a drink. They accepted, quenched their thirst, and went away. Ya Martha said later, "It was the Lord who told me to do this."

Ya Martha was sitting on her veranda one day when she saw a throng of people leading a man through the village to the chief. The man was bound with ropes around his hands and waist. Martha became as sad as if one of her own family were being treated this way. She hurried to the chief's compound where she found the man tied up tightly.

"What has this man done that you're treating him like this?" she asked.

"This is Bokari," they answered. "He's crazy, and he's been trying to burn houses and hurt people!"

"Please, loosen his ropes a bit," Martha begged.

"No! If we do that, he'll escape." And they put Bokari in jail.

Martha would not give up. "Have you given him anything to eat?" she asked one of the court messengers.

When he said no, Ya Martha asked if she could bring Bokari some food. The messenger agreed. Pa Bai, Martha's pastor-husband, agreed also.

So Martha prepared some food. Before she took it to the prisoner, she asked the Lord to bless it.

Later, Bokari somehow got hold of a machete. He refused to give it up, and everyone was afraid to try to take it from him. Then Bokari said, "Call that mama." The court messenger came for Martha. When she arrived at the jail, Bokari gave her the machete.

Most of the time, Bokari behaved like a wild man. He pounded the jail doors and yelled so loudly that the people on the other side of the village could hear him.

On the third day of his imprisonment, Ya Martha brought him some rice and soup. For the first time, he said, "Thank you."

Martha told him, "Say 'Jesus.'" She repeated Jesus' name to him many times, but he refused to say it. So each time she went with food, Martha would say, "Bokari, say 'Jesus, thank you.'"

Finally one day he said, "Jesus, thank you." Then he asked Martha, "Ya, who are you?"

And she answered, "The Jesus I'm telling you about has saved me, and he'll save you too."

From the time he said Jesus' name, Bokari's mind was calmed, but the people didn't believe it. They still feared him.

Martha asked if Bokari could leave the jail and stay with her family. Some of the people began to think that she was the crazy one.

Ya Martha prepared a bed on the veranda. She took Bokari there and said, "In the name of Jesus, you will lie down here for the night. Jesus will keep you."

After he lay down, Martha heard him say, "Oh, Jesus, help me." In the morning, he said, "I didn't wake up once during the night. Thank you, Jesus." Jesus' love had come to Bokari through the love of Ya Martha.

CHAPTER 20

Don't Punish Them!

When he was seven years old, Adamu Dogon Yaro's father took him on a six-day journey away from his village. At the school where his father left him, Adamu spent eight years studying and learning by heart the Muslim holy book, the Koran. If he knew all of the Koran, he could be an important person and religious leader in his village. His village was in north central Nigeria. His tribe, the Fulani, were all Muslims, and Adamu knew of no other religion.

Because of his father's death and a dispute with his uncle and older brothers, Adamu did not return to his village. He worked in another town as a servant and as the Muslim teacher of the town. As the Muslim leader, he gave the call to prayer five times a day. He was in charge of the worship services at the mosque. And he made charms with verses from the Koran for people to wear to protect them from evil.

Now Adamu had two teenage friends who were studying in a school run by missionaries. Adamu first heard about Jesus from them. He learned a new language—Hausa—so he could read the New Testament. Finally,

Adamu, the Muslim teacher, decided that he had been on the wrong track. He left his old religion (Islam) to become a Christian.

Because he began to follow Jesus, Adamu received hatred and misunderstanding from his wife and his fellow Fulani tribesmen. But Adamu never turned back. God led him to go to Bible school to become a missionary, and to find a Christian wife, Jumai. Many times his faith led him into situations where his life was in danger.

After Bible school, Adamu and Jumai went to the village of Nishama where a tribe of fetish worshipers lived. This wild tribe lived by hunting. Whenever they caught a big animal, such as a leopard or a bush cow, everyone would celebrate by feasting and getting drunk.

For a whole year, Adamu and Jumai found no friends in the village. Their neighbors were hostile to them and didn't want them there. Everything Adamu did made them suspicious.

One day when Adamu was walking along, a man working in his yard greeted him. Adamu answered the greeting and added, "You should repent of your sins and believe on the Lord Jesus."

"What do you mean, saying that to me? Say it again, and you'll see what happens!" threatened the man.

Adamu repeated, "You should repent of your sins and believe on Jesus."

The man rushed out of his yard and struck Adamu on the face. "Now, say it again!" he threatened.

Adamu said, "You should repent and believe on the Lord Jesus that you might have eternal life."

Suddenly, other village men appeared, carrying clubs. All the bad feelings they had held against Adamu for a year went into the beating they gave him.

Finally Adamu regained consciousness. He got up and limped along, aching and bruised, to the town of Kagoro to report his beating to the authorities. The authorities there told him he should go farther to report it to the district headquarters.

The officer at the district headquarters called the attackers to come to a hearing. After listening to the reports, he told Adamu, "You should not have called like that to the man in his own yard. You should have called him out to talk to him."

"I did not wish to disturb him in his work," Adamu replied.

"My judgment is that they will each have to pay you a fine," the officer decided.

"I don't want them to be punished," Adamu said. "I didn't report them for that. I only want you to warn them. I don't mind about my own injuries. These men need to be more careful, or the next time they may be charged with murder. Please, don't fine them."

"They must be fined," said the officer.

Besides their fines, the guilty ones also received a warning. Before long, the whole village had heard of Adamu's pleading that the men not be fined. What could this mean? They had hated him and beaten him—and he only wanted the judge to warn them! The very men who beat him now wanted to be his friends. Adamu saw that while his preaching alone was ineffective, his actions had touched them deeply and had made an influence on them.

CHAPTER 21

I Shall Not Be Moved

Yona Kanamuzeyi was surprised and not sure he wanted the job. After two years in Burundi studying at the theological college, he had expected to return to the congregation he had been pastoring before in Northern Rwanda. Now the church had asked him to go instead to work among the refugees in the southern part of Rwanda.

The fighting in Rwanda between the Tutsi and Hutu tribes had left many people homeless. In 1960 the government began settling a number of them in the region of Bugesera. Because of its crocodile-infested rivers and swampy land, few people lived there. Yona knew that to work there would not be easy, but he also knew that God was leading him to do it.

Yona did have energy and patience—and a close fellowship with God. His practical ideas and ability to organize made him an ideal person for his new job at Maranyunda.

One of his jobs was to receive the supplies which arrived for the refugees: powdered milk, medicines, bedding, clothing. He had to see about using money gifts to buy food, seeds, and young banana and coffee trees to plant.

There never seemed to be enough and some tried dishonestly to get more than their share. He needed the wisdom of Solomon and the mind of a detective.

The first time Yona met with the Christian refugees, they gathered under a large tree for protection from the sun. To encourage them, Yona read from the Bible about how the Lord was their shelter and shade. He talked about how they were to be like strong trees near the nourishing stream. According to Psalm 1, such trees remain firm in times of storm or in times of dryness. Then he taught them to sing the chorus, "Just like a tree planted by the waters, I shall not be moved."

How happy Yona was when he could have a house! His wife, Mary, and their children could come to live with him. The other people could not understand the way Yona and Mary loved each other; he did not treat her like a slave! The women would ask Mary, "Doesn't he ever beat you or curse you?"

"No," answered Mary. "Instead, sometimes he asks my forgiveness, and I ask his. And Jesus forgives us. Then we pray together."

About 1961 some Tutsi refugees, who had fled to neighboring countries, began to use terrorist tactics. They hoped to overthrow the government of Rwanda and bring back their king. These terrorists were called "Inyenzi" or "cockroaches." As the situation worsened, any Tutsi could be suspected of being Inyenzi.

Though destruction and fighting were common in many places, the people in Bugesera district continued to live peaceably. But in late 1963, rumors flew everywhere that the Inyenzi were going to invade Rwanda. Twice the Inyenzi actually attempted invasions from Burundi, but the

Rwandan army pushed them back.

From that time on, the army began arresting anyone suspected of Inyenzi connections. Some of those arrested were killed. Many of the hundreds who were put in prison died from the crowded conditions.

Yona continued his work. One time he ignored the curfew to find and bury the body of a church worker who had been shot in the street. He encouraged the Christians who also, in spite of the curfew, gathered in his house to pray.

In January 1964, a friend came to Yona and said, "You're going to die."

"Why do you say that?" asked Yona.

"For two reasons: your belief in the Word of God, and for the way you love everyone."

Yona said, "Those two things—the Word of God and the love of God are two things I can't live without."

He told Mary about this, and they prayed together. "God, you called me and sent me here," Yona said. "You know me, the days I've already lived and the days which remain. If it's your will to call me home, I'm ready."

Thursday morning, January 23, in family worship, Yona read Psalm 27, verses 3 and 4: "Though a host encamp against me, my heart shall not fear; though war arise against me, yet I will be confident. One thing have I asked of the Lord, that will I seek after; that I may dwell in the house of the Lord all the days of my life."

At 7:30 that evening a Jeep stopped in front of Yona's house. Six soldiers came in, surrounded Yona, and said, "We want to question you." Yona and Mary knew that when the soldiers took someone at night, they were never seen again.

As he left, eight-year-old Wesley said, "You'll hurry back, won't you, Papa?"

"Yes, I'll hurry," said Yona.

Two other prisoners were taken along in the Jeep. The soldiers drove north until they crossed the bridge over the Nyaborongo River. Then they made the prisoners get out of the Jeep and put all their possessions on a pile. Before he laid down his journal, Yona wrote in it, "We're going to heaven." Then he made a note of the amount of church money he had at home. He placed his journal, his key, and a few francs on the pile and asked that they be given to his wife. "You'd better pray instead," said a soldier.

Yona prayed, "Lord, you know I haven't done anything against the government. I pray that you will help these people who don't know what they're doing." As the hands of the three prisoners were tied behind their backs, they sang together. "There is a happy land far, far away."

Then the soldier led Yona away, leaving the other two behind. As he went, he sang.

There's a land that is fairer than day.
And by faith, we can see it afar.
Where the Father waits over the way.
To prepare us a dwelling place there.

They took Yona to the bridge, shot him, and threw his body into the river. The stunned soldiers hardly knew what to do next. They had never seen anyone die singing. They released the other two men and threatened them to tell no one. One of them—Andrew—later shared this testimony of Yona's last moments.

CHAPTER 22

If Someone Must Die, Kill Me

The village of Lazaro, beside Lake Albert and surrounded by the Blue Mountains, was usually a peaceful
spot. But in the late 1960s, there was no peace for Lazaro.
The Belgian Congo had become the Congo Republic but
had not yet become Zaire. A group of rebels, called Simbas,
was fighting against the new government, killing the
people and looting their villages. Now they had arrived at
Lazaro.

"Someone from this village must die!" shouted the rebel
leader to the village people. The people were afraid—just
what the rebel soldier wished.

With an ugly sneer, he continued. "When we come to a
new village, we always kill someone to show that we are
the only authority."

The people waited silently. As the leader slowly looked
them over, he noticed two strong young men standing to
one side.

"Say, you two," he shouted. "Why not one of you? The

only thing is to decide which one."

The people were horrified, and some of the women began sobbing. One of the Udubre brothers, leaders in the village, was going to be killed!

Then their father, an old gray-haired man, walked up to the rebel leader and spoke. "Please, I beg you. Don't kill either one. They both have families who need them. Don't kill them. They are my sons."

"Someone must die!" shouted the soldier. "I won't listen to you. Get out of my way!" And he gave old Lazaro Udubre a push.

"Wait!" said Lazaro. "If someone must die, let it be me! I'm old and I've lived my life. I'm a Christian and I know that I will go to heaven where it is more beautiful than anywhere on earth. So kill me."

The rebel chief listened, but could hardly believe what he was hearing. He didn't know what to think. Finally, he said, "All right. Since you want to die, it will be you." He ordered two of his men to tie Lazaro up and put him in the truck. His two sons rushed up and kissed their father. Even they could hardly understand what their father was willing to do for them.

"Don't worry about me," their father reassured them. "And don't try to change my mind. I know what I'm doing. We'll see each other again one day in heaven with Jesus." Before he could say any more, the rebels took off through the forest in their truck.

When they reached a clearing where the rebel camp was located, the soldiers ordered Lazaro out of the truck. Around him he saw bodies scattered over the ground. He saw a row of men and boys lined up. He saw soldiers reloading their guns.

"So this was where I am going to die!" he thought.

"Wait a minute," called the chief to the firing squad. "This man here says he's a Christian. He has offered to die instead of his sons. He ought to be able to preach. So, old man, you have one minute to preach to these men before we shoot them. That should be interesting!"

"How can anyone be so cruel, and make fun of death and of God's word?" thought Lazaro. But God was giving him the chance to speak about him to these prisoners, so he walked over to them.

"Listen," he said. "Many of you know about Jesus. But if you don't believe in him, it's not too late. Remember the thief on the cross beside Jesus? He believed and was saved just before his death. Believe in Jesus and he will save you, too. Jesus said, 'I will not reject any one who comes to me.'"

Several of the prisoners bowed their heads and sobbed out their prayers. While they were praying, they were shot and fell to the ground dead. Later, two other rebel trucks arrived at the clearing with groups of villagers. Two more times Lazaro was able to tell the men of Jesus before they were killed. For some unknown reason, he was not shot that day.

When night came, he was pushed inside a hut. He could not sleep, however, because his mind was filled with the horrors he had seen.

The next day was like the day before. Groups of condemned men arrived and Lazaro preached to them. Then there were groups of bodies to be buried.

Each morning Lazaro thought, "I'll surely be killed today. How can I stand to see any more of this butchery?" But no. Had the drunk rebels forgotten that their "preacher" was also one of the prisoners who was to die?

One day a rumor spread through the rebel camp. The government army was coming near to destroy the rebels! Now, it was the rebels who were afraid. They jumped into their trucks and disappeared into the forest, leaving Lazaro alone in the clearing. He was free!

Later the Christians of the village, once again at peace, gathered to hear God's Word. When they heard how Jesus died in their place, they understood the words better. For there with them was the living example of Lazaro, who also had loved enough to volunteer to die in his sons' place.

CHAPTER 23

Love Can Heal

It had been nearly 100 years since the church began in Uganda with the death of a group of young Christians. (See "You Can't Burn Our Souls.") Archbishop Janani Luwum and the rest of the church were planning to celebrate this centennial anniversary in 1977.

The celebration never took place. Dictator-president Idi Amin's persecution of the church was increasing. Many of the bodies fed to the crocodiles or beheaded by Amin's assassins were those of Christians. Six of them were the young men who were to play the parts of some of the early martyrs in a drama to celebrate the 100th birthday of the church. They were found slain in a field near the memorial to those who had died earlier. As for Archbishop Luwum
. . . .

On February 1, 1977, men from Amin's Special Forces arrested a man and tortured him for five days. They wanted to make him name people who "might have been" working against the government. They forced him to give more and more names until in desperation he suggested the name of the archbishop.

A few days later in the middle of the night, Luwum was awakened by someone banging on the door. Seeing a man who looked injured, he opened the door. Eight men with rifles who had been hiding burst in, shouting, "Show us the weapons!"

"What weapons?" asked the startled archbishop.

"There are weapons in this house! Show us!" they cried. "Take us to your bedroom!" They woke his wife, crawled under the bed, climbed into the closets, looking everywhere. Then they searched the children's rooms.

Luwum said, "Our house is God's house. We pray for the president. We pray for the security officers no matter what they do. We preach the gospel and pray for others. That is our work, not keeping arms!"

They continued their search, looking in the study, under the communion table in the chapel, in the sacks of grain in the storeroom, in the guest rooms, in the bathrooms, and in the parked cars.

After searching over an hour without finding any weapons, they said, "Open the gate so we can leave."

Luwum's wife said, "Why don't you go out the way you came in?" for they had broken down the fence to come in.

But Luwum said, "We are Christians. We have clean hearts, and as a witness, I will open the gates for them."

That same night another bishop had his home searched and he was taken away for questioning.

The bishops, knowing this was a serious matter, met together to write a statement of their concerns to President Amin. The bishops personally delivered copies of this fearless but loving statement to the president, his cabinet, other religious leaders, and the Defense Council.

Luwum was able to talk to Amin. He said that he did

not protest the searching of his house. However, he did object that it was done at gunpoint and in the middle of the night. "Don't worry about a thing!" said the smiling president. "I'm going to invite all the bishops to come, and we'll talk it over!"

That evening both the radio and the newspaper said that weapons had been found near the archbishop's house and that he was involved in a plot!

The next day, February 16, all religious leaders were ordered to come to the Conference Centre at 9:30 in the morning. They arrived outside the building to find almost the whole army and most of the government officials gathered there. There was also a display of Chinese weapons—supposedly those that the archbishop had smuggled in.

The guards brought out some prisoners who had been tortured. These prisoners testified that the church leaders had smuggled these arms in because no one would suspect them. Throughout the day, the religious leaders had to listen to speeches and accusations. When the vice-president asked what he should do with the churchmen, the soldiers shouted, "Kill them! Kill them!"

They waited all day in the sun with no food or water. Finally at 3:30 one of the military officers said, "You can go home and do your work." As they were leaving, the guard said to Luwum, "Not you, archbishop. The president wants to see you in that room."

No one else was allowed to go with him. Two of the bishops—Wani and Kivengere—waited at his car for him. At 5:00 p.m. they tried to question the guards. The guards told the bishops to leave, saying, "He is still busy. We will bring him home. You get out of here." Finally, at gunpoint, they were forced to leave.

When they told the archbishop's wife this news, she went with her driver and the car back to the Conference Centre. She said to the guard, "I want to go in and find out about my husband." The guards almost shot the driver and she had to leave with no news.

Although no one outside knew it, the archbishop was already dead. Amin had asked him to sign a confession and he had refused. When he began praying aloud for his captors, Amin ordered the soldiers to shoot him. When they refused, Amin shot the archbishop himself. Two of Amin's cabinet members were executed at the same time. Then trucks were driven over the bodies so that people would believe the story broadcast on TV the next day—that the three men had died in a car accident.

On the screen they also showed a picture of the wrecked car, but people knew that it was a car that had been in a wreck a week before. Festo Kivengere, one of the bishops who was able to flee from Uganda soon after Luwum's death, said, "I love Idi Amin. I have never been his enemy. Anyone who loves humanity must seek the constructive, reconciling way. God did it. Who am I to stray from his way? So that's why I love Idi Amin. As long as he is alive, he is redeemable. Love can heal. Pray for him."

CHAPTER 24

A Miracle of Love

Thomas loved the Lord, and he loved people. His neighbor across the path not only hated God, he hated everyone who loved him, including Thomas. This man was so full of hatred that one night he sneaked over to Thomas' hut and set fire to its thatched roof. Fortunately, Thomas discovered the fire in time to put it out and save his children.

That did not discourage this hateful neighbor, however, and the next two nights he tried again to burn Thomas' hut. Again Thomas was able to put out the fire in time. Even though Thomas knew who was doing this to him, he continued to treat his neighbor with love and respect. This only seemed to increase the man's hatred.

One night he came creeping over the path again for another try at burning Thomas' house. It was windy that night, and before Thomas could extinguish the fire, the wind carried some sparks over to the roof of the neighbor's hut.

As soon as Thomas had managed to put out the fire on his own roof, he rushed across the path to help his neighbor. Together they were able to save the house, but Thomas' hands and arms were severely burned. Other neighbors went and told the chief the story, and the chief put Thomas's neighbor in prison.

The next evening, Thomas went as usual to his church. The visiting speaker was Corrie ten Boom, an elderly Dutch lady who had been imprisoned by the Nazis in World War II. She noticed Thomas' burned hands and asked him what had happened.

When she heard his story, she said, "It's a good thing your neighbor is in prison. Now, you won't have to worry about what may happen to your children and your house."

"That's true," said Thomas, "but I feel sorry for him. He's a gifted person, and now he is shut up in that awful prison with all those criminals."

"Then, let's pray for him," suggested Corrie.

Thomas knelt, raised his burned hands to God and said, "Lord, I wish that this man would become one of your children. Lord, I pray for his release and for a miracle in his heart. I pray that we will become brothers in Christ and will be able to preach to our tribe together. Amen."

Corrie thought, "Never before have I heard a prayer like that one!"

Two days later, she visited the prison and spoke to the inmates. Thomas' neighbor was among them, listening attentively. At the end of her talk, Corrie asked whether anyone wished to become a Christian. Thomas' neighbor was the first to raise his hand.

After the meeting she told him about Thomas' injuries and about the prayer he had prayed. Tears came to the man's eyes. He nodded his head and said, "Yes, one day we'll do that together—preach to our tribe."

When Corrie told Thomas the news, he praised God and said, "You see. God has performed a miracle! Nothing is too hard for him."

CHAPTER 25

I Cannot Follow Two Paths

Salah lived in Algeria where nearly everyone is Muslim. In Koranic school, he learned to read the Muslim holy book. He also heard his teachers denounce Christians. They told how Christians had fought and killed many Muslims to claim the land of Palestine in those wars called the Crusades.

His teachers said, "Christians believe there are three Gods! They believe that Jesus is God's Son! How can God have a Son? The Koran tells us that Jesus is only a great prophet."

This made Salah curious. He wanted to find out more about Christianity. Once he found a Bible and read it in secret, beginning in Matthew. He read Matthew 5, where Jesus talks about the poor, the peacemakers, and the persecuted being blessed. When Salah read this, he believed that the Bible was God's Word, not the Koran. But he knew of no one who could help him understand the Bible. When he came to the Lord's Prayer in Matthew 6, he prayed it to God. Then he added, "O God, send me someone to help me understand your Word."

Nothing happened. Some time later, his father was ill
and sent Salah to a Christian hospital for some medicine.
There he heard the doctor speaking from the Bible. He
went back on Sunday, and the doctor took him to the hospital chapel where Salah heard people singing and praying
in his own Arabic language. That day he received the Lord
into his heart.

When he was older, he began to work for the Bible So-
ciety as a traveling Bible salesman. His job was to go from
village to village selling Bibles. Sometimes he would set up
a little stand at the weekly markets.

At one village, someone bought a New Testament and
took it directly to the mosque. The leader, the imam, and
the man who had bought the New Testament hurried
toward Salah with angry looks on their faces. Angry people
began to crowd around them, ready to do whatever their
leader asked them.

Salah told God he was ready to die if necessary. Then he
began to explain the books he was selling. He pointed out
that the Koran accepts parts of the Bible, such as the Law,
the Psalms, and the Gospels.

Finally, the imam told the people it was all right to buy
them. In seven minutes Salah had sold all the books in his
two suitcases!

Salah's real troubles with the police began after the war
in 1967 between Israel and its Arab neighbors. Being an
Arab country, too, Algeria didn't trust any foreigners who
might be friends of Israel. Salah, of course, was an Arab,
but people distrusted him because they thought that Christianity was a foreign religion which had no place in a Muslim land.

Many times the police questioned and arrested him.

Often he used those times to talk about his faith. Once the police asked if he sold his books to Jews, Christians, or Muslims. Salah answered, "I am introducing you to the Bible as something for everyone—not a Jewish book or a book on politics. I sell it to all who feel their need of one."

The police tried to get him to tell them the names of other Christians. They said, "You are an Algerian citizen. You must help your country!"

Salah answered, "I am an Algerian citizen and a Christian. I want to help my country, but as a teacher."

They told him, "If you won't cooperate with us, we will take away your bookselling permit and keep you from getting any other kind of work. Come back tomorrow and turn in your permit."

Salah did as he was asked, but the police inspector said, "Salah, you're a good man. We only wanted to scare you because you were obstinate and wouldn't work for us. You can continue selling books."

Another time when he was arrested, they asked him, "If Israel attacks us, would you fight with us or with the Jews?"

Salah replied, "I'm not for either side; I'm for Christ. War comes from Satan."

Then the Algerian police inspector sent for some Muslim religious leaders to try to persuade him to give up his Christian faith and become a Muslim again.

Salah told these leaders, "If I wanted to lie to you, it wouldn't be hard for me to say that I am a Muslim. But I am a Christian, and I can't be both at the same time. I can't follow two paths. There is only one path to God."

The police inspector then asked Salah to repeat the Muslim creed, "There is no God but God, and Muhammad is his prophet." These words would make him a Muslim.

Salah refused.

The inspector told one of his officers, "Place your machine gun at his head and fire if he will not say the creed." The man placed his gun at Salah's head.

Salah answered, "I am not afraid. I will be happy to leave this world and be with God."

Instead of commanding the officer to fire, the inspector asked Salah if Christians prayed. When Salah said yes, the inspector asked him to pray so he could listen. Salah prayed for the poor and the sick, for the Algerian government, and for God's help in his own difficulties. Salah was not shot, but he was kept in jail.

The next day they questioned him from morning till night. They tried to trap him with trick questions. Then they prepared a false report which spoke against some missionaries. They promised him money, a job, and influence if he would sign it.

Salah answered, "I have never met anyone richer than Jesus Christ. Working for him is better than any job you can offer me."

The police finally let him go. But they made it impossible for him to work in Algeria and impossible for him to leave the country. So he fled by a secret route and went to France, knowing he would never be able to return to his native land.

Now Salah is witnessing among the hundreds of thousands of North Africans who live in France where they have gone to work. Although far from his home, he is still helping Africans to find their Savior.

CHAPTER 26

Anger Will Just
Destroy You

Many people believe that violence is the only way left for blacks in South Africa. Ezra does not agree.

Ezra is a Christian in South Africa living in the black homeland, Transkei. He says, "We need a goal that's greater than fighting. Peace must be the end goal. If it's not, then what we end up with will be no better than what we have now. You can't let yourself stay angry. That doesn't help. Anger will just destroy you."

It's not that Ezra doesn't have any reason to be angry. He works for the Transkei Council of Churches.

One day he was taken from his office by the security police. For three months no one heard from him. Finally, he was charged, and after three months was tried and acquitted. The judge could find no evidence to convict him of harboring wanted persons or recruiting people for the banned liberation movement. His ear still gives him trouble as a result of police beatings.

This was not Ezra's first experience in prison. The Security Police first came after him when he was only 20 years old. He had written some articles about happenings in Transkei. To avoid trouble, he went to live in Lesotho. At age 24 he returned to Transkei from Lesotho. He brought with him many books from all over the world which he had received through membership in the National Peace Council.

Ezra said, "I wanted to share these with my friends in Transkei. Some of them were becoming involved with underground movements and sabotage. I thought they should know more about the international struggle for peace and justice. But the police found me with my books and arrested me.

"They accused me of having been to the Soviet Union for training in sabotage. They hit me and threatened me. One of them said, 'We'll use the same methods against you that the Russians taught you to use against us.' I said they could check and find out that I had just been in Lesotho. But they wouldn't believe me.

"While I was in prison, a white Dutch Reformed pastor came to visit me. He said he waited a long time to come, because he thought I'd probably hate him and not want to see him. But I told him, 'No, I want to pray with you. I am a Christian, and I can pray with you as a fellow Christian.' I also told him that apartheid was wrong for that very reason—Christians attacking their fellow Christians."

Ezra was released in 1967 after three years in prison. The next year a friend asked Ezra if he knew of any housing available for another friend. Ezra found him a room.

Eight months later Ezra was arrested for harboring a terrorist. The man had come from Tanzania where antigovernment guerrillas are trained, but Ezra hadn't known that. He and nine others were tried under South Africa's Terrorism Act. Ezra was sentenced to ten years in prison.

The first year was difficult. Ezra says, "We were all in Pretoria Prison, in solitary cells. The warden really hated us. He said we were worse than criminals. I have never seen such hatred as I saw in that man's eyes.

"We were fed only three spoonfuls of porridge a day. We were so starved we looked like those photos of Jews in the Nazi camps. It was too painful to sit up because of stomach cramps. So, we just lay on our bunks all curled up. We ate toothpaste; another prisoner who worked in the prison store felt sorry for us and brought us toothpaste."

After that year, the other nine years he spent on the Robben Island prison for political criminals seemed a relief.

How can Ezra tell of these experiences with a smile? What has made him able to come through these trials without bitterness or hatred? He says, "Those people who beat me and mistreated me did it because they really believed I was a terrorist and a threat to them. Otherwise, I don't think they would have been able to do those things. So you can't be angry at them. You have to understand them as people who have a wrong understanding."

As a church worker, Ezra involves himself with victims of South Africa's unjust laws, with families of political prisoners, and with refugees. He encourages the churches of Transkei to ask hard questions about laws and the treatment of prisoners. He also has a dream—to form again a South African Peace Council.

He says, "We need a Peace Council with groups all over South Africa. Some people say that talking about peace is useless—that we need to fight. But they need to see that to talk about peace doesn't make us work less for freedom, because it is only through justice that peace can come." In spite of the suffering, Ezra still has the courage to love.

Sources

1. "Martyrs africains d'hier et aujourd'hui," *Pirogue no. 29*, Editions Saint-Paul, Issy les Moulineaux, France, 1984. *Les premiers Martyrs chrétiens* by Lydie Huynh Khac-Rivière, Editions Saint-Paul, 1977. *Aux lions les Chrétiens* by Eugene Porret, Editions "Le Phare," Belgium, 1985.
2. "Martyrs africains d'hier et aujourd'hui," *Pirogue no. 29*, Editions Saint-Paul, Issy les Moulineaux, France, 1984. *Les premiers Martyrs chrétiens* by Lydie Huynh Khac-Rivière, Editions Saint-Paul, 1977.
3. *L'afrique sein et berceau du christianisme* by Cyprien Arbelbide, Tiassalé, Abidjan, Côte d'Ivoire, 1976. *Peace Be with You* by Cornelia Lehn, Faith and Life Press, Newton, Kans., U.S.A., 1980.
4. *The Story of the Copts* by Iris Habib el Masri, Middle East Council of Churches, 1978.
5. *The Story of the Copts* by Iris Habib el Masri, Middle East Council of Churches, 1978. *L'afrique sein et berceau du christianisme* by Cyprien Arbelbide, Tiassalé, Abidjan, Côte d'Ivoire, 1976.
6. *The Story of the Copts* by Iris Habib el Masri, Middle East Council of Churches, 1978.
7. "Le livre qui ne voulait pas brûler," by Evelyne Maire and

Solomon Andria in *Découvertes no. 4*, Groupes Universities Bibliques and Ligue pour la Lecture de la Bible, Abidjan, Côte d'Ivoire, 1983.

8. *Histoire des missions ét églises protestantes en Afrique occidentale des origines à 1884* by Jean Faure, Editions CLE, Yaoundé, Cameroon, 1978. *The Early Church in Africa* by John P. Kealy and David W. Shenk, Oxford University Press, Nairobi, Kenya, 1975. *Christianity in West Africa* edited by Ogbu Kalu, Daystar Press, Ibadan, Nigeria, 1978.

9. *L'afrique sein et berceau du christianisme* by Cyprien Arbelbide, Tiassalé, Abidjan, Côte d'Ivoire, 1976. "Martyrs africains d'hier et aujourd'hui," *Pirogue no. 29*, Editions Saint-Paul, Issy les Moulineaux, France, 1984.

10. *Samuel Morris and the March of Faith* by Lindley Baldwin, Dimension Books, Minneapolis, Minn., U.S.A., 1942.

11. *A Prophet of Modern Times: The Thought of the Prophet William Wadé Harris* by David Shank, University of Aberdeen, Scotland, 1981.

12. *Témoins camerounais de l'Evangile* by Francis Grob, Editions CLE, Yaoundé, Cameroon.

13. *Black Samson* by Levi Keidel, Christian Life Missions, Wheaton, Ill., U.S.A., 1975. *Simon Kimbangu* by Marie-Louise Martin, Editions du Soc, Lausanne, 1981. Reprinted by permission from *Christian Life* magazine, Christian Life Missions, 396 E. St. Charles Rd., Wheaton, IL 60188.

14. *L'orphelin au coeur blessé*, autobiography of Ndomikolayi Massake, CEDI, Kinshasa, Zaîre, 1972.

15. *Ils n'ont pas résisté* by Anni Dyck, Editions "Le Phare," Belgium, 1977.

16. *Courez avant la nuit* by W. Harold Fuller, Lausanne, Switzerland, 1968. Adapted by permission of SIM International.

17. *Courez avant la nuit* by W. Harold Fuller, Lausanne, Switzerland, 1968. Adapted by permission of SIM International.

18. *Only One Weapon* by Harold Adeney, Ruanda Mission, London, 1963.

19. *Dramatic Stories for Missionary Programs* by Marie Lind, Baker Book House, Grand Rapids, Mich., U.S.A., 1972.
20. *Black Nomad* by Eva Doerksen, SIM, New York, 1969. Adapted by permission of SIM International.
21. *Pardonne-leur* by J. E. Church, Editions des Groupes Missionnaires, Vevy, Switzerland, 1967.
22. *African Heroes of the Congo Rebellion* by Hal Olsen, Kesho Publications, Kijabe, Kenya, 1969.
23. *I Love Idi Amin* by Festo Kivengere, Fleming H. Revell, N.J., U.S.A., 1977. *Battle for Africa* by Brother Andrew, Fleming H. Revell, N.J., U.S.A., 1977.
24. *Tramp for the Lord* by Corrie ten Boom, Fleming Revell, Old Tappan, N.J., U.S.A., 1974. Used by permission.
25. *God's Messengers* by Marian Hostetler, Mennonite Publishing House, Scottdale, Pa, U.S.A., 1985.
26. "Anger Will Just Destroy You" by Judy Zimmerman Herr, *Gospel Herald*, Oct. 1, 1985, Mennonite Publishing House, Scottdale, Pa, U.S.A.

The Author

Marian Hostetler teaches school at Concord West Side Elementary School in Elkhart, Indiana. She has taught there for 16 years and had taught earlier in her hometown of Orrville, Ohio.

Marian received her B.A. in elementary education from Goshen (Ind.) College and an M.S. in education from Indiana University, Bloomington, Indiana.

Writing is a hobby for Marian. She has written five books, including *Mystery at the Mall,* released in 1985 by Herald Press.

She has also written materials for children, including *God's Messengers*, a mission study series commissioned by the Mennonite Board of Missions. It is available from the Mennonite Publishing House.

Marian collected and adapted the stories for *They Loved Their Enemies* during a nine-month assignment for Mennonite Board of Missions in West Africa, 1985-86. Her assignment included research on the training needs of the independent churches of Benin. In Côte d'Ivoire, she worked on a project about the life of Prophet Harris. She also was employed half-time by CPE, a Christian publishing company.

Marian served as a teacher in Algeria with the Mennonite Board of Missions (MBM) from 1961-70 and as an editorial assistant in Information Services of MBM from 1958-60.

PEACE AND JUSTICE SERIES

Edited by Elizabeth Showalter and J. Allen Brubaker

This series sets forth briefly and simply some of the important emphases of the Bible on war and peace and how to deal with conflict and injustice. The authors write from within the Anabaptist tradition. This includes viewing the Scriptures as a whole as the believing community discerns God's Word through the guidance of the Spirit.

Some of the titles reflect biblical, theological, or historical content; other titles in the series show how these principles and insights are practiced in daily life.

1. *The Way God Fights* by Lois Barrett.
2. *How Christians Made Peace with War* by John Driver.
3. *They Loved Their Enemies* by Marian Hostetler.

The books in this series are published in North America by:

Herald Press
616 Walnut Avenue
Scottdale, PA   15683
USA

Herald Press
117 King Street West
Kitchener, ON   N2G 4M5
CANADA

Overseas persons wanting copies for distribution or permission to translate may write to the Scottdale address listed above.

Then we make
a  of the
LIST   BIRDS
we see.

If it's  we play
RAINING
different games in
my 🪆 .

ROOM